FINISHING LINE PRESS
www.finishinglinepress.com

Fabric Heart:

A Collection of Contemporary Introspective Sijo

poems by

Tamara K. Walker

Finishing Line Press
Georgetown, Kentucky

Fabric Heart:

A Collection
of Contemporary
Introspective Sijo

ISBN 978-1-63534-947-4 First Edition

ACKNOWLEDGMENTS

This chapbook is dedicated to the passionate and eclectic network of poets, editors and commentators who continue to write, publish and develop original East Asian poetry in English today, with appreciation for all of the organizations and individuals whose translational, educational and creative efforts contribute to keeping the sijo tradition alive.

In gratitude to the diligent handful of journal editors that have accepted my poems for publication over the years—especially those who have so generously encouraged my nascent forays into Asian forms with kind words and astute feedback.

Publisher: Leah Maines
Editor: Christen Kincaid
Cover Art: Pixabay
Author Photo: Tamara K. Walker
Cover Design: Elizabeth Maines McCleavy

Printed in the USA on acid-free paper.
Order online: www.finishinglinepress.com
also available on amazon.com

Author inquiries and mail orders:
Finishing Line Press
P. O. Box 1626
Georgetown, Kentucky 40324
U. S. A.

Table of Contents

for all who celebrate dignity

Author's Note

Among the various short, traditional East Asian poetry forms that have been cross-culturally adapted in modern times from their original linguistic and historical contexts, the Korean sijo has long especially captivated me. With much less restriction than haiku and more explicitly defined boundaries in English than the still-nebulous tanka, the sijo is comparatively spacious, offering the poet considerable accommodation for elaborating upon a broad range of themes through figurative elements such as overt simile, subtle metaphor and rhetorical questions. Traditionally arranged in three lines of 14-16 syllables—each prosodically subdivided into two sections and four phrases of varying length—sijo structure provides just enough formal constraint to effectively frame and channel sprawling currents of perception and imagination, with sufficient room in which to convey intricate contemplation that illuminates far-reaching truths from a perspective of concrete if generalizable experience. The open and flexible though grounded nature of sijo—which has transcendently emerged from its ancient and musical origins in no small part thanks to the efforts of skilled translators over several decades—affords the form a remarkable sincerity that appealed to me as a young writer thus far otherwise primarily inclined towards experimental, darkly ambiguous and obliquely bizarre modes of expression, adrift in increasingly amorphous literary and psychoemotional realms.

Integral to the essence of many if not most extant sijo is a multifaceted encapsulation of symbolic connections between enduring external realities (e.g., natural environment and phenomena, political and interpersonal circumstances, etc.) and internal landscapes emotional and philosophical. In this way, whether they take an "inside-out" or "outside-in" approach to doing so, sijo often bridge and combine direct, arresting observation culled from life's plexus of fluctuating rhythms with emotive subjectivity, giving rise to a template for gentle lyricism that lends itself well to deeply personal, ambivalent introspection during difficult and transitional periods. Around the time that the sijo included here were written, I found myself meandering in a somewhat uncomfortably indistinct phase of my creative life reflective of, and to a major extent resultant from, significant upheaval (to put it mildly) in my mundane and intimate ones. Fortuitously, it was during a similar stage that I had discovered sijo nearly seven years earlier and began constructing my own. Just as it had back then, the form's narrative qualities and elegant cadences—as well as the comfort of writing within a solid foundation of definite yet pliable guidelines—felicitously supplied a much-needed outlet for my suddenly confessional impulses and ruminations.

Centered on an interpretation of the sijo as a compositional, sentimental inner dialogue with oneself, the 45 poems in this small collection strive to incorporate salient aspects of the timeless fluidity, seasonal allusions and sensibilities of classical sijo in translation while suffusing this ancient form with traces of vaguely contemporary symbols, scenarios and distinctly divergent attitudes, adhering closely to syllabic convention. Sprinkled with occasional anachronism both stylistic and technological, they seek to communicate an integrated assortment of moods and impressions unspooled from the intense, disjointed tumult of short-lived relationships, frantic self-reassessment and stark lessons learned in the contrition of a painful divorce. With regard to sijo traditions, they are mainly inspired by and perhaps most congruous in spirit (though of course dissimilarly situated in the types of relationship dynamics portrayed) with the relatively sparse though impactful and adroitly metaphorical body of love-themed sijo by anonymous poets—at least a fair number of whom were ostensibly women, suggested to have been muted by the strictures of Confucian hierarchy—as well as talented *kisaeng* such as Hwang Jini. Many examples in this vein are of a cleverly feminine, acutely confessional and almost brooding tint unusually accessible to contemporary readers unversed in Korean studies; I recommend them highly, and can only aspire to faintly echo a fraction of their sophistication and dexterity. If sijo itself is the loom on which the poems in this abbreviated chapbook were crafted, this subset of symbolic and emotionally forthright sijo about love, relationships and solitude is the pattern that germinated their coloration and design.

Composed in layers of varying accessibility, and interwoven in light but vital continuity, the sijo collected here comprise the fibers of the titular fabric—sometimes as loose and translucent as amateur knitting, and elsewhere as dense and tightly compressed as felt. Throughout I have attempted to modestly demonstrate what pioneering sijo poetess Elizabeth St. Jacques once candidly stated in an early article about the form in a Western context: "No matter how the North American vision might alter sijo in English, it is hoped we honor its place of origin and basic concept, and consider it an instrument of international communication and good will." Enjoy.

I. Irreparable Tear

a fragile bird once splashed love across my fractured memory
awakening I find no such thing, and so I stand here—
swallowing delayed hope in white capsules, and chasing it with tears

tidying office supplies, I'm struck with well-deserved sadness
my organization skills, it seems, have finally reached their peak
but how could I ever use pads on which you wrote apologies?

"CARTRIDGE LOW" the warning says as I try to print her picture
when we painfully unfastened, this machine stayed with me
in another time, it prints love notes in fading magenta ink

belatedly unpacking months later, I suddenly feel weak
poison bubbles in my chest are merely a hollow afterthought
still, I can't bear redundant remnants of a searing almost-life

words in my throat crystallize into ashen amethyst fragments
growing uncomfortably on everyone's paralyzed eardrums
obsolete radio silence goes unheard when I speak of you

noxious nightly dreams punch purple vacancies in sheets we once shared
your absence reflects holes from within that always existed
without you to wrap around them, what will they consume but the world?

the battery in my phone became impossible to charge
each new cable I bought failed to help retrieve our messages
just as then, I can only breathe through perfumed white lies for so long

tasteless strawberries bring to mind days when we purchased every fruit
the sundresses I wore back then have had their color all washed out;
I never was successful at dyeing cotton garments

in between winter and spring, the weather seems to admonish me
each snowflake a frozen corpuscle of unexperienced joy
it is like that, I suppose, when all that warms you is your coat

pages behind mellifluous poetry absorb damage
marred with ghostly impressions, they cushion typebars' impact
as you became a backing sheet, the platen of our passion was scarred

"once upon a time," your bedtime stories to me sometimes began
I listened and slept as our time unknowingly slipped through our hands
fairytales don't end happily when dragons are born from the maid

II. Drifting Lint

adrift in empty granite rooms, I g(r)asp for misted landmarks
words, images and sounds misalign in decaying holograms
while I seek the merciful eternal in lavender geodes

flecked with lilac ambivalence, I transformed my new apartment
erasing marks left on these underground walls in sunlit silence
my subterranean conscience is not so easily spackled

walking through wet autumn leaves, there is an occasional crunch
insightful calm lands on my shoulders with the last elusive moth
yet tomorrow, when needed, it will spiral into the cold street

getting lost in an area where the holiday lights were sparse
I squinted at familiar street signs, strangely to no avail
only peering through tinted lenses did I find my way home

succumbing again to seclusion, I fail to comfort myself
slogging through heavy yellow syrup, the anguished days blur by
syrups are saccharine, though, and now I just swim through bland aether

ascending charcoal hills at midnight in an olive-green dress
self-subterfuge drifts in my ears with these minor notes of love worn
all to diminish static after main channels went off-air

alone for days, I press my heels into laundry-scented landscapes
only one star visible in the cloudy absence of the moon
particles of fresh detergent scatter across my fabric heart

today it snowed; yesterday the sun melted the sky with summer
oversleeping peacefully, newly frigid air awakens me
and so I'm left sipping iced watermelon tea in my sweater

brewing sugar cookie-flavored tisane long out of season
I hope that its milk thistle will optimize my medication
for then, I can recapture how I felt at that time in two ways

viscous distractions interrupting discipline so easily—
I resolved this month to dissolve them in the acid of routine
is it possible, I wonder, to turn honey into oil instead?

III. Safety Pins

rainbow clay sprout covered with gray dust in the shadows of my desk—
it appears to have wilted, its turquoise stalk bent with doleful months
now that I notice, it's just growing sideways, angled slightly up

artificial bouquets forever bloom from a nondescript vase
requiring neither light nor water, they remain vivid
how I envy that, as a blossom that withers if you turn your back

decorative holes in my fan might render it ineffective
when overdressed for tepid temperatures, it barely cools me
I'd rather mask my red face, though, beneath obsidian lattice

unused staples stuck in a row like each one of my metaphors
to attach the sheets of this life, they must be warped by pressure
then again, most symbols are designed to fold in upon themselves

the bitter taste of zopiclone strikes my throat like distant thunder
under and over these unspoken breaths, it shrouds ire with rain
muting the acidic pulsations beneath my eroding ribs

lingering and gazing at spent tea leaves as through a monocle
their murky morphing mass contains little to portend better days
at least I'm extending this moment, with the fragrance of jasmine

unfinished projects sit neglected like untended friendships
someday, I tell myself, these opportunities will sparkle
until that day arrives, I can never, ever let them go

reels of cassette and adhesive tape form a crumpled zebra
both divorced from their purposes, they wind around highlighters
but pens to write the future are not at the bottom of this box

IV. Loose Patches and Lost Buttons

your presence a vapor condensing on me only late at night
I strive halfheartedly to resist your roiling timid pull
but we are like asteroids, tugged into orbit upon approach

after intoxicating neon nights, you left me in terror
the link between our hearts split into a thousand separate threads
threads that strangled me as I tried to weave them together for you

holding a dandelion to the camera, "a flower for you"
I imagined the seeds traveling the whole distance between us
in a way, they did—to plant beautiful weeds in your gardened self

in that initial daze, I saw the map to my core through her eyes
inky villains coalesced around what they were born to protect
in the end, not even the gentlest clear solvent can dispel them

V. Dye and Pattern

I empathize with tiny spiders dangling from fine silk threads
each day subject to natural winds, and hoping no one will breeze past
if only I had eight eyes, to track and avoid everyone's steps

some sunlight is always there, but all my golden robes are tattered
I hide behind drapes, glancing out in narrow filtered bursts
trapped, in the heavy two-tone cloak of this nighttime mentality

of all flowers, petunias detach from the plant quite easily
yet they do not press well, becoming only dull violet tissue
so too are the emotions I tried to preserve inside books

tape binds together the denuded face of a twice-shattered clock
only the second hand still functions, passing over shards and cracks
I've always passed time like this, futilely cycling through instants

finding promising reflections of new ways of being
I file them wistfully away with past ephemera
even burning alive, it is awkward to extinguish these flames

reflecting on malfunctioning solar panels for weeks on end—
warm rays glaze their surface so brightly, yet they energize little
similar is my motivation, though perhaps I'm just facing north

when childhood unicorns are misplaced, it is as if they charge
is it so painful to be impaled on gleaming sequined horns?
far less so, than archives of a present that never came to be

VI. Seams and Sewing Machines

lying on the carpet twirling colorful scarves above my head
I imagine a blanket so vast as to enfold the whole world
draped like a maternal hug, repairing all our torn, frayed fibers

glimpsing the splintered aftermath of yet another frenzied storm
amidst dried droplets of sapped agony, a strange thought comforts me
somewhere, in fierce despots' desks,
rest sweet poems they wrote as children

reading about metaphysics while waiting for an appointment
I update my worldview before updating my paperwork
farewell, Nietzsche—your madding chaos is dissipating

using this diary years later for a different theme
I tear out several filled pages, lamenting the loss of space
though like us as we mature, it carries more meaning with less

unbearable cacophony vibrates this clear plastic ceiling
enclosing us all, it is discolored with layers of filth
yet the softest piano notes can break through, and bathe us in light

Further Reading/Resources

For detailed and thorough explanations of the nuances of sijo structure as well as the history and heritage of the form, I refer the reader to the excellent repository of resources compiled and hosted by the Sejong Cultural Society (available as of the time of this writing at https://www.sejongculturalsociety.org/writing/current/resources/sijo_links.php), as well as the introduction to Richard Rutt's exemplary translation of classical sijo, *The Bamboo Grove: An Introduction to Sijo.* Another volume that contains a brief explanation of sijo as well as translations of classical examples is *Sunset in a Spider Web*, by Virginia Olsen Baron and illustrated by Minja Park Kim:

Rutt, Richard. *The Bamboo Grove: An Introduction to Sijo,* University of Michigan Press, 1998.

Baron, Virginia Olsen. *Sunset in a Spider Web*, Holt, Rinehart and Winston, 1974.

A few examples of books containing original sijo in English are listed below:

Kim, Goeng Pil. *The Stone to the Cloud: Sijo Poetry Composed in English,* CreateSpace Independent Publishing Platform, 2015.
St. Jacques, Elizabeth. *Around the Tree of Light: A Collection of Korean Sijo*, Maplebud Press, 1995.
McCann, David Richard. *Urban Temple: Sijo, Twisted & Straight*, Bo-Leaf Books, 2010.
Park, Linda Sue. *Tap Dancing on the Roof: Sijo (Poems)*, Houghton Mifflin Harcourt, 2007.

For those interested in original English sijo, few active journals currently exist dedicated to publishing them, either in print or online. However, I recommend *Eastern Structures* (Nocturnal Iris Publications), which includes poetry in many Eastern forms, and contains a sijo section. *Sijo: an international journal of poetry and song* (a project of the Korea Text Initiative), "is devoted to publishing germinative poetry, art, and song that claims to participate in the sijo tradition." (http://www.sijopoet.org).

Tamara K. Walker is an emerging poet and writer of short fiction, usually of an experimental, irreal, surreal, slipstream or otherwise 'unusual' variety. One of her short stories, "Camisole" *(The Conium Review, Vol. 4)*, was a 2015 Pushcart Prize nominee; the same piece was also nominated for inclusion in *The Best Small Fictions 2016*. Her fiction has appeared in *The Café Irreal, A cappella Zoo, The Conium Review, Melusine, Peculiar Mormyrid, ink&coda, three minute plastic, Apocrypha and Abstractions, Gay Flash Fiction* and the anthologies *Life is a Roller Coaster, Switch (The Difference)*, and *Storm Cycle 2014*, published by Kind of a Hurricane Press.

Her tanka have appeared or are forthcoming in *Ribbons, Eucalypt, GUSTS, LYNX, Atlas Poetica, Moonbathing, A Hundred Gourds, bottle rockets, Star*Line*, and *Scifaikuest*. She is a member of the Tanka Society of America (TSA). Her sijo have appeared in *LYNX, Eastern Structures, Scifaikuest* and *Spaceports & Spidersilk*, and her other poetry has been published in *Lavender Review, indefinite space* and *The Ghazal Page*, among various other journals and zines. *Fabric Heart* is her first chapbook.

She is a third-generation native of Colorado, where she currently resides, and may be found online at http://tamarakwalker.weebly.com. She is interested in and has some limited academic background in conceptual metaphor theory, which often influences her work and approach to creative writing and literary analysis.

www.ingramcontent.com/pod-product-compliance
Lightning Source LLC
LaVergne TN
LVHW041526070426
835507LV00013B/1854
9781635349474